FEAR

THE OTHER *F* WORD

Bessie Stewart-Banks Ed.D.

Conscious of the Heart Publishing, LLC
Atlanta, Georgia
www.cothpublishing.com

FEAR THE OTHER F WORD by Bessie Stewart-Banks Ed. D.

Published by   Conscious of the Heart Publishing, LLC
P.O. Box 1452
Redan, Georgia 30074

Unless otherwise indicated, all Scripture quotations are taken from the Holy Bible, New Living Translation, copyright © 1996, 2004, 2007, 2013, 2015 by Tyndale House Foundation. Used by permission of Tyndale House Publishers, Inc., Carol Stream, Illinois 60188. All rights reserved.

Scripture quotations marked (NIV) are taken from the Holy Bible, New International Version®, NIV®. Copyright © 1973, 1978, 1984, 2011 by Biblica, Inc.™ Used by permission of Zondervan. All rights reserved worldwide. **www.zondervan.com** The "NIV" and "New International Version" are trademarks registered in the United States Patent and Trademark Office by Biblica, Inc.™

Scripture taken from the New King James Version®. Copyright © 1982 by Thomas Nelson. Used by permission. All rights reserved.

Scripture quotations marked KJV are from the King James Version of the Bible.

ISBN-13 978-0692107720
ISBN-10 069210772X

Library of Congress Control Number 2018942318

Printed in the United States of America

DEDICATION

This book is dedicated to people who desire to move pass fear and step out on faith to explore the limitless power of their creative ability and journey into new unchartered territories.

ACKNOWLEDGEMENTS

To Danielle Rome-Briggs thank you for your insight and professional editing service. Dimitrinka Cvetkoski thank you for expertise, creativeness and professionalism for the construction of the cover to this book and throughout the entire process. Without your support and assistance, the publication of this book would have not been possible. I also would like to express my gratitude to Minister Christine Norman and Elder Regina Nunnally, J.D. for your positive remarks and encouragement.

DISCLAIMER

This book was written with the intent of providing information to the reader based on research and biblical principles. The content within this book by no means serve as professional or expert advice. The author and publisher shall have no liability or responsibility to any person or persons regarding harm or loss that may occur directly or indirectly by the information contained within.

FEAR

In a sea of the unknown we press forward

to understand what we don't know,

searching for answers to our inadequacies

to define our misconception of others.

To comprehend why we limit ourselves and

choose to stay in the same place year after year

never daring to explore new adventures or territories.

Suddenly time invites herself into our life

saying there is no more room for improvement

or correction because we allowed Madame Fear

to enter in our space.

We now walk hand and hand with fear

never discovering the many blessings

that God had waiting for us

and the lives we could have touched.

Fear is now our consciousness.

-Dr. Bessie Stewart-Banks

TABLE OF CONTENT

PREFACE

How often have you dreamed a dream, desired to do something that no one else has ever done before? Have you ever dared to explore uncharted waters in a professional realm, but for one reason or another you retreated? Instead you decided to settle for a more simplistic, regulated and mundane way of living filled with regret, indecisiveness, and reluctance. Because of your decision and hesitation to not step out on faith into the deep sea of life you developed an unauthorized relationship with fear, failing to understand that there are repercussions to forming this type of relationship.

As you journey through the pages of this book, you will gain a full understanding of why some people step out in the deep sea of life and accomplish their goals in life, while others allow fear to hold them hostage and rob them of their hopes and dreams.

CHAPTER 1

What is Fear?

Fear is thought to be one of the most unsettling emotions that can drive a rational person out of character and far removed from their normal Morteis Operatories (aka M.O.). In retrospect, fear can be the largest crippling and debilitating factor that hinders most people from striving to reach new heights in life. Beyond the scope of fear being a crippler, it is viewed as the number one hindrance that stops many people from moving into their destiny, stepping out in faith to pursue their hopes and dreams and valuing the uniqueness of others.

Consequently, fear is considered an unrecognizable component of Christendom. It is suggested that fear is an emotion that no Christians should neither entertain nor develop a covenant relationship with. As it is stated in 2 Timothy 1:7, *"For God had not given us a spirit of fear and timidity, but of power, love and self-discipline."* Fear is much like the stepchild to human emotions and it should be avoided at all cost. The only fear that we should have in life, is the fear of the Lord. We are instructed in Proverbs 9:10, to have a holy reverence in favor of Elohim (God, the creator). I digress, however, to suggest that fear does offer an explanation as to why some people behave the way they do, why they do what they do when they do it; as well as why they don't do what they should do when they know they need to do it.

Fundamentally speaking, fear is an infectious and corrosive disease that robs many people of their peace of mind and joy. Fear also invades the lives of people to the extent they walk around in a constant state of paranoia, always thinking that someone is out to cause them harm or believing that something bad is going to happen to them or to their love ones and that something that was terrifying that occurred before in their life will occur again.

FEAR vs. FAITH

Fear and faith vacillate between two dimensions of thought: unbelief and belief. One form of thinking battling to be number one in a person's life as well as the supreme thought process for that individual's belief system. I would like to frame this movement between the two dimensions of thought as the Spiritual Pendulum Effect (S.P.E.). On one side of the Spiritual Pendulum Effect there is the dimension of fear which we will address first. On the other side of the Spiritual Pendulum Effect we have the dimension of faith, which we will discuss in detail later.

The greatest challenge that arises as we attempt to describe fear is locating an adequate definition that pen points the true and factual meaning of the word. According to *Strong's Concordance*, the Hebraic term for fear is *daag*. Daag means to be anxious and afraid.[1] As it relates to an individual's emotional state, fear is synonymous to anxiety, worry, stress and doubt.

In other words, fear can be described as scared of the unknown or a situation that presents itself as a challenge or threat to an individual who is attempting to move out of their comfort zone. The *American Heritage College Dictionary* describes fear as *"a feeling of agitation and anxiety caused by present or imminent danger."*[2] Fear can be viewed as being afraid of something or someone.[3]

In certain aspects fear is having an unusual loss of courage.[4] Some psychologists, however, belief that fear is an emotional response to a certain form of threat or danger.[5] Hence, fear is a counterproductive emotion that kills, destroys, robs, corrupts the minds of sane people, presents situations as disastrous, distorts the truth and taints a person's relationship and fellowship with God.

As stated earlier, faith is the opposite dimension to that of fear within the Spiritual Pendulum Effect. It is noteworthy to mention that the tenets of faith are captured in every type of religious belief system. However, for the sake of this topic we will focus exclusively on the tenets of the Christian faith. When you think about faith the key descriptive words or terms that should come to mind are: trust, hope, assurance, belief, conviction and the full confidence in a doctrine, principle, or thought. Since faith plays an intricate role in every Christian's daily walk and commitment to God and his son Jesus Christ, it is vitally important to not only provide satisfactory terms that describe faith but also offer a straightforward and detailed explanation as to what faith is.

To be more explicit, faith is not playing it safe or having an alphabet backup plan. Faith is being able to move forward into your hopes and dreams without having full knowledge or an understanding as to how the results will pan out. Faith is believing that something will happen or take place without having any evidence that it will come into existence. All in all, faith is an action, a one-dimensional movement toward Christ. As stated in Hebrews 11:1 (NLT), *"Faith is the confidence that what we hope for will actually happen; it gives us assurance about things we cannot see."*

There are various resources that offer plausible descriptions for faith: 1.) having confidence or trust in a person or thing; and 2.) believing in God or in the principles or the knowledge of religion. Based on the definition given by most dictionaries, faith is having a strong religious feeling or belief system.[6] Nevertheless, no matter which definition a person chooses to express what they believe to be a representation of faith, the main point to faith is having a strong conviction and relationship with a higher power.

Although the Spiritual Pendulum sways back and forth in either direction, from fear to faith; the body of Christ must stand flat-footed, committed and unapologetic as their faith gravitates toward God. Faith must be allowed to manifest and be reflective in their daily walk. As it pertains to fear, fear is not our friend and it should always be denounced and rejected every time it rears its ugly head in our lives. Hence, the word of the Lord in Matthew 6:24 (NLT) states, *"No one can serve two masters. For you will hate one and love the other; you will be devoted to one and despise the other...."* Based on this passage of scripture, it is therefore, strongly proposed that people in general take the high road and live life by faith and not in fear.

CHAPTER 2

Origins of Fear

Fear is an unfortunate reality, yet one must ask "where does it come from?" Inevitably, from time to time, fear will have a tendency of showing its ugly head in a person's life. No two people will be confronted with the same type of fear. The severity of fear and how it is handled will vary from person to person. There are several degrees of fear and they derive from various sources. According to research evil forces and spirits, involuntary hearsay, life circumstances, societal conflict, preconceived views and ignorance are the top six origins of fear.[7]

Evil Spirits and Forces

Evil spirits and forces are ranked number one for the top six origins of fear. This component of fear explains why ungodly spirits and forces appear in a person's life, oftentimes unexpectedly. Evil spirits and forces are more than often transferred to individuals by way of someone else's words, deeds or they simply creep into someone's thoughts or imagination. These evil spirits and forces emanate from Satan, the author of lies and the archenemy of God.

The main objective of these evil spirits and forces is to throw people off their course in life and to plant seeds of deception in their mind. The planting of such seeds only leaves the perception that life is bad, and it will not get any better than it already is. Moreover, satanic spirits and forces are also sent to cause people to think and believe that the something they are hoping will occur in their lives will not come into existence. Subsequently, these same spirits and forces pose as distractions to keep people from accomplishing the purpose and plan that God has placed on everyone's life.

Involuntary Hearsay

Involuntary hearsay, like that of evil spirits and forces, is considered one of the origins of fear. This origin of fear not only perpetuates the spirit of discouragement but serves as a distraction mechanism. Involuntary hearsay more than often stems from the negative remarks, opinions and suggestions of naysayers. Naysayers are those persons who never have anything good to say and see life from a pessimistic viewpoint.

Additionally, naysayers are like secret agents of the enemy, whose main objective again is to distract us and lead us down the road of disbelief and doubt. However, fear, in this instance, can arise in an individual's life only if they allow themselves to listen and believe the words that flow out of the mouths of naysayers. Believers of Jesus Christ should never allow themselves to accept which oppose truth to come into their spirits or mindsets. Believers must refuse to be pulled away from the divine purpose that they were created to accomplish in the earthly realm.

Life Circumstances

Life circumstances are another origin of fear that can appear in a person's life. Life circumstances can have a profound effect on a person's physical, mental, emotional and spiritual well-being. Loss of employment, financial indebtedness, health problems, marital issues and the loss of a love one, are examples of life circumstances that can impede a person's sense of security.

When an individual must deal with a multitude of complexities in life such as debt, unemployment, sickness, rebellious children and marital strife there is a tendency to get sidetracked and bogged-down. They may then endure the loss of focus which weakens and stagnates their faith walk, to the point their prayer life dwindles, and they begin to believe there is no hope for their situation. However, the word of the Lord in Psalm 121:1-2 (KJV) instructs us to "…*lift* [our] *eyes unto the hills, from whence cometh* [our] *hel*p. [For our] *help cometh from the Lord, which made heaven and earth."*

Societal Conflict

Societal conflict is another origin of fear. Societal conflicts take place in every community throughout the world. More than often societal conflict arises from issues within the dynamics of families, violence (one person imposing harm on another person) between groups of people and government entities, as well as discord amongst neighboring countries.

For instance, societal conflict can come into existence when a person is assaulted by another person, regardless to if it was a family member or a total stranger; when there is a breach of trust between an elected official and citizens within a community; or the inability of world leaders to come into agreement regarding a certain matter. In either instance, when no viable resolution is offered and those who are involved rely on their own strength and wisdom, the propensity of violence will occur which in turn causes some people to become hateful and cynical; while another segment of people is drawn into being fearful and timid. However, Hebrews 13:6 (NLT) states, *"So we can say with confidence, the Lord is my helper, so I will have no fear. What can mere people do to me?"*

Preconceived Views

Preconceived views are the fifth origin of fear and stem from one person prematurely judging another person or a situation before gaining all the information they need to make a sound, informed and intelligent conclusion. There is a tendency for some people to judge an entire group of people based on a singular horrific event or act, imposed by a depraved or demented individual, such as a drive by or mass shooting that might have occurred within the boundaries of a city. Because of that terrible act or event, it is therefore presumed that everyone in that community is the same as the people who performed the act. However, the basis of this notion is far from the truth. It is dangerous to assume that the behavior or action of one person, or even a small percentage of people within a specific group are always detrimental. These overgeneralizations are not a true depiction for the entire community.

Consequently, the danger comes into play when people begin to live their lives in a constant defensive mode, being overly suspicious of everyone in their immediate surroundings. In turn, the suspicious and presumptuous thoughts or viewpoints of one person about another person can eventually cause one to act just like, or better yet worse, than the person that is under suspicion. We are reminded in Matthew 7:1-2 (NLT), *"Do not judge others, and you will not be judged. For you will be treated as you treat others. The standard you use in judging is the standard by which you will be judged."* Therefore, we must be careful to not form preconceived notions about people and mistreat them.

Ignorance

The final origin of fear is ignorance. According to research, ignorance arises from the lack of wisdom and knowledge about a subject matter, person, or groups of people. Simply speaking ignorance stems from someone being misinformed about a topic, a group of people, culture or religion. As it is stated in Hosea 4:6 (NIV), *"…my people are destroyed from the lack of knowledge."*

Ignorance is a dangerous component of fear. Ignorance is hazardous because there are some people who will gravitate toward a specific ideology or concept without fully understanding what it is all about. There is a far too persistent failure to do their due diligence to research and obtain as much information as they possibly can about the idea before making a conscience decision to dislike something or someone. Ultimately, ignorance out of fear and vice versa causes some people to act and behave in a manner that is oftentimes detrimental to themselves as well as to others.

No matter what direction fear tries to come against you whether it is by evil spirits and forces, the words of naysayers, acts stemming from life circumstances, societal conflict or the behavior of ill-informed individuals, we the children of light must remain steadfast and unmovable in our faith and walk with Jesus Christ. For it is stated in Jeremiah 1:8 (NLT), *"And don't be afraid of the people, for I will be with you and will protect you. I, the Lord have spoken!"*

CHAPTER 3

Fear in Action

In many modern-day societies, there are countless people who are confronted with a plethora of personal issues that they must deal with daily. The task, however, becomes somewhat challenging when they must navigate through an array of deep-seated personal issues, in conjunction with the social-ills that plague various areas within urban and rural communities. There are some people who find that dealing with life struggles and societal problems overwhelmingly stressful and cumbersome to the point they position themselves to live out life in a reactive mode verses living life in a proactive mode. As a result, individuals of the reactive nature become part of the problem instead of part of the solution.

People who live in a constant reactive mode in terms of fear are often prone to displaying behaviors that are considered violent and irreparable. For example, someone physically harms another person because they have different viewpoints or outlooks on life. The actions in this example come with a price. The loss of freedom for the person who committed the act and for the individual who was harmed, a loss of trust for humanity.

Subsequently, there are psychologists who suggest that people who choose to act out or express their fears do so because of xenophobic biases. [8] Xenophobic biases are a by-product of xenophobia, a condition that is caused by a person being afraid of a person or group of people because of their cultural background or ethnicity. There have been studies conducted on xenophobic notions and based on those studies it is implied that people who act out due to fear do so because of circumstances that are beyond their immediate control. In view of these studies, violence is the main culprit that reactive people resort to when acting out of fear.

Acts of violence are not just portrayed in the form of physical harm by one person against another person; violence regarding fear can be acted out through hateful rhetoric. Hateful rhetoric comes into play when someone belittles another person by speaking unkind words that are of ill intent, not factually based and no substantial evidence is presented in support of their statement or argument. The action of speaking hateful words is the most damaging of its kind.

For instance, think of a person, no matter how old they are, being subjected to verbal ridicule on a consistent basis by another person over a long period of time. This repeated verbal harassment and assault could potentially lead to the person bullied becoming a bully themselves or at the worst, committing suicide. Henceforth, since the tongue is considered the sharpest body part, we must always be mindful of the words that we use toward one another. Scripture explicates in Proverbs 18:21 (NLT), that *"the tongue can bring death or life; those who love to talk will reap the consequences."*

Above and beyond fear being portrayed through acts of violence and hateful rhetoric, fear can also be filtered through the vehicle of the mistreatment of others. As humans, we have the tendency to treat others in the same manner that we were treated or even worse. The mistreatment of others is noticeably evident when it comes to someone being treated negatively, with discontentment, rudeness and any other behavior that is deemed to be offensive and harmful.

A good example of the mistreatment of others can be gathered from the example given earlier about the bullied becoming the bully. This behavior aligns with the old cliché that "hurt people hurt people." The mistreatment of others is an act where the word of God in Luke 6:31 (NLT) distinctly warns us, *"Do to others as you would like them to do to you."* Therefore, it should serve as a reminder that if we don't want people to mistreat us we must be careful as to how we treat them, so that the mood of reciprocity for the mistreatment of others will not visit our door step.

Retreating into isolation is another result of fear being in motion. Living in a state of isolation and far removed from people is hazardous and poses as an interruption to the normalcy of regular societal interaction with people. According to psychologists this type of behavior or way of living is closely related to social anxiety. [9] Typically, when people live this way they do so because they feel that being in isolation provides a safety net, serves as a type of security blanket or a measure toward being safe from external factors.

Even though fear can transform and manifest itself in multiple ways in the lives of those who are enslaved by it, it is proposed that every precautionary measure be taken so that those persons who are entangled with this destructive emotion will embrace the courage necessary to free themselves from a bondage that seemingly robs them of their hopes, dreams, productivity, peace, soundness of mind and joy. Even so an individual's inability and failure to combat their personal fears will eventually cause them to experience complications that will unknowingly affect their health, mental, spiritual and physical well-being.

CHAPTER 4

Results of Fear

Fear is such a crippling emotion that it blocks the creativity and positive outlook a person has about life. Fear has a way of inadvertently causing people who are enslaved by it to experience various challenges in the areas of their physical health, their personal relationship with God, their path toward spiritual growth, their level of living, and the goals they desire to obtain in life.

Physical Ailments

The most challenging aspect of fear that can impede a person's attempt to live out their best life in a way that is meaningful and productive stems from how well they can deal with stress and anxiety when it appears. There are studies which suggest that if fear (i.e. stress or anxiety) exists in a person's life over a long period of time, it could negatively impact the person's health, and can possibility cause physical ailments. The top four physical ailments that could affect a person's health include: hypertension (i.e. high-blood pressure), tension headaches, insomnia, and depression.

Hypertension is one of many physical ailments caused by a presence of fear and stress in a person's life.[10] The onset of hypertension can have an adverse effect on the health to the extent that some people develop heart disease and as a result experience a heart attack or stroke. Although hypertension is considered the main physical ailment it is also thought that some people have developed irregular sleep patterns, known as insomnia, because of not effectively coping with fear or stress. [11] the lack of sleep can and will have a negative impact on a person's overall physical health. If a person doesn't get the appropriate amount of sleep their immune system will be susceptible to weakening.

Likewise, high levels of stress associated with fear can cause tension headaches. For example, a person can experience a tension headache because they are overly stressed that something horrific is going to happen at work, uncontrollable life circumstances concerning their family or the inability to pay their bills in the manner they desire. In contrast to those experiencing physical ailments, there are many people who deal with depression as it relates to fear. Depression can appear in several ways, however, when it comes to fear it will show up in the form of low emotions coupled with bouts of anxiety. According to research there are millions of people who suffer with depression daily.[12]

When you think about fear and depression their impacts are congruent; they limit or restrict a person's ability to function at full capacity and what society deems as normal. People who are fearful in life and are battling poor health, inadequate sleep and mental stress will eventually experience some form of physical ailment if the problem is not properly addressed.

Bond Breaker

The essence of fear being present in the life of the believer poses as a threat to the bond and intimate relationship they have with God and his son Jesus Christ. The existence of fear in the believer's life also causes them to disconnect from the Holy Spirit (the one who was sent to be a comforter until Jesus returns). Fear not only tends to interrupt the flow of the Holy Spirit in the believer's life, it prevents them from receiving inspirational and godly downloads from heaven and the ability to fully trust and believe in the sovereignty of God.

Nevertheless, anytime a believer fails to reject fear, and allows it to impede their relationship with God, there will be the propensity for them to turn around and blame the very creator that created them along with placing blame on others for their misfortunates in life. However, the true ownership for why fear causes chaos in a person's life rests on the shoulders of those who befriend it. Hence, if people embrace fear they will always live beneath their God-given privilege and limit the ability to build healthy and vibrant relationships with both God and man.

Spiritual Growth Inhibitor

In conjunction to fear being able to limit the relationship that a person has formed with the Creator and the development of friendships with new people, fear also has the tendency to leave a person spiritually paralyzed. The inhibitive nature of fear not only creates situations in which distrust and doubt arise, but it leads some people to believe that God is not who he says He is.

However, there is a line of thought that allows fear to misguide individuals in the way they think, to the point that they are skeptical of God and his people. This type of thought process causes the person to question the authenticity of the man or woman of God. Additionally, fear has a way of blocking a person's ability to gain the wisdom and knowledge of God's word. Without the wisdom and knowledge of the word of God there is no way for a person to comprehend the truth of his word.

Besides fear hindering a person's understanding of the word of God, it has the potential of stopping people from praying and creates an environment where the person no longer seeks the presence of God when hopeless circumstances arise in their lives. Thus, fear poses such a threat to the overall spiritual growth of a person that it forces them to take their eyes off God and focus more on what they are afraid of. Subsequently, if fear can hang around in a person's life like a theft in the night, it will always block, steal, and kill the spiritual growth of the believer.

Complacent Living

Oftentimes, people who decide not to live out their lives in a meaningful way do so because of their fear factor. They are comfortable with living a mediocre life. They do not welcome new ways of doing things or meeting different people. People of this caliber do not like or accept change. Furthermore, people of this nature believe that by doing things the same way, year after year, somehow protects them from unforeseen events. Moreover, people who choose to live their lives in complacency and within the constraints of familiarity have not truly lived a fulfilled life and stubbornly refuse to change.

Dream Killer

Fear can be a dream killer, especially when it is led by procrastination. Even the most ambitious and successful people can be robbed of a prosperous life if they allow fear of the unknown to creep into the stream of accomplishing their goals and aspirations. The way fear can invade a person's space is in the form of their thought process or by negative words expressed by family members, close friends, or associates; they may believe that these goals and dreams that they desire to fulfill are impossible. Fear is not only considered a dream killer, but it is also a deterrent that causes many people not to experience any of the good things that life has to offer them and the realization of the blessings that God has already granted them.

In comparison, fear is like worry and stress and has the potential of being disastrous to a person's overall well-being. Fear, like any physical illness, can have a lasting effect on a person's health, spiritual growth, relationship with Jesus Christ, their perception about life, and the goals they have established to accomplish in life. Although the results of fear will appear as negative and unfavorable in a person's life, they do have the option to change. As stated in 1 Peter 5:7, we should *"cast all* [our] *anxieties on him because he cares for* [us]*."*

Therefore, it is suggested that if anyone is feeling a sense of anxiety or stress and has noticed that they have been coexisting with fear, they should make a conscious decision to trade fear for faith. The trade-off in the end will prove to be more beneficial to a person's life.

CHAPTER 5

Conquering Fear

Fear can be one of the greatest challenges that a person has to overcome in life when they have succumbed to its grip. For that reason, it is necessary for a person who is living with fear to discover the best reasonable solutions available to them that will help them in gaining freedom from this paralytic emotion.

Here are some helpful tips that people who are confronted with the effects of fear can take into consideration when attempting to overcome it:

Regular Visits to a Physician

As it was previously mentioned, fear can manifest in the human body in such a way that it can adversely affect a person's health. The various health problems that can arise because of fear can appear in the form of hypertension, tension heartaches or insomnia. Regularly scheduled visits to the doctor's office can help alleviate most of the health problems that people experience while being a preventive measure to uncover any potential health issues that could emerge.

Maintain Healthy Eating Habits

Generally, when it comes to a person who suffers from stress related illnesses such as hypertension, it is more than likely that when they visit their physician for an annual check-up they are asked a series of questions regarding their health. Some of the typical questions that they are asked fall within the categories of their eating habits, sleep pattern and exercise routine. Although an individual's sleep pattern and exercise routine are crucial components to understanding their health status; knowing a person's eating habits provides some indication to the physician as to what is going on in the person's body and possibly how the foods they are consuming are contributing to their health and moods.

It has been suggested by some health professionals and nutrition experts that there are certain foods that help with the lowering of high-blood pressure, cholesterol levels as well as boost a person's mood. Therefore, incorporating healthy foods into a person's diet and maintaining a healthy lifestyle is another way to help combat illnesses associated with stress and anxiety.

Incorporate a Regular Exercise Regimen

It is suggested that when a person exercises their body releases a chemical known as endorphins. Endorphins are neurotransmitters that are transmitted throughout the human body. [13] It has been proven that the release of endorphins brings about a shift in a person's mood and decreases their stress levels. Based on this information, incorporating a regular exercise regimen into a person's daily schedule is beneficial to a person's overall health in several ways:

1.) Helps with weight loss
2.) Promotes a healthy heart
3.) Enhances the functionality of the brain
4.) Lowers blood pressure
5.) Encourages positive self-imagery
6.) Improves sleep

Spend time in Prayer

Spending time in prayer with God has a way of erasing any forethought of doubt, worry or anxiety that may be lingering within a person's mindset or spirit. Praying to God brings about peace, clarity and has a way of changing how a person perceives their problem or issue. Furthermore, seeking the face of God through prayer rekindles a person's hope, their outlook on life, and the promise that there is a better tomorrow.

The most important thing that a person should know about praying to God is that beyond telling him what their concerns are, they must remember to be thankful for what he has already done in their life. According to Philippians 4:6-7, *"don't worry about anything, instead, pray about everything. Tell God what you need and thank him for all he has done. Then you will experience God's peace, which exceeds anything we can understand. His peace will guard your hearts and minds as you live in Christ Jesus."*

Meditate on the Word of God

To combat any issue in life, like fear, it would be necessary for a person to discover what the word of God says about their situation in life. Meditating on the word of God provides us with some key elements:

1. **Guidance**
   - Rationale for action
   - Timing for action
   - Methods of action

2. **Direction**
   - Specific destination
   - Path to reach destination
   - Awareness of the journey not merely a destination

3. **Clarity**
   - Revelation of truth
   - Arrival at definitive decision
   - Discernment throughout the process

Simply speaking, the word of the God (the Bible) is our blueprint on how we should live. Nonetheless, after a person understands what the word says about the issue they are dealing with and the answer they sought after regarding that issue, it is then important for them to know how to apply it.

Apply the word of God

Application of the word of the God to life's situations, combined with daily prayer and meditation on the word of

God, is another effective way of combating fear. For the word of the Lord in Psalm 119:105 states that, "[the Lord's] *word is a lamp to guide* [our] *feet and a light for* [our] *path."* It is important to remember that the application of the word of the Lord is not a one-day effort. The application of the word must be done continuously and on a regular basis, otherwise, it will be ineffective. Therefore, once an individual has discovered what scripture says about their circumstance they should put it into use immediately, trusting and believing that what the word says is true and factual and will not return to them void.

Surround yourself with positive people

Being surrounded by positive people has a way of changing a person's perspective about life. The very nature of positive people is so infectious and catchy, it is impossible for someone to be around them and the positivity is not transferred to others. People who are optimistic and upbeat about life are more than often change agents and view conflict in life as an indicator that something great is going to happen for them. Seemingly positive people always see good, even in bad situations.

Discover the source of your fear

As a rule of thumb, it is common that before a solution can be developed for any type of problem, it is wise to first examine the issue in its entirety to get to the root cause of the problem so that the problem can be properly addressed. This rule of thumb holds true for real life scenarios. For instance, a young woman has a hard time maintaining lasting relationships for an extended period with the men she dates. One would think that based on the young woman's inability to maintain a committed relationship with the person she's dating, she then must have an issue with trusting men.

However, the underlying cause to the non-existence of a lasting relationship may be deeper than just the young woman's lack of trust men. One rationale for this young woman's problem may be rooted in the fact that her father may have abandoned her as a child and she is now afraid that if she becomes too involved with a man, then, he too will abandon her. Another rationale for the young woman's lack of trust in men may stem from a bad experience she is still harboring within her mind and spirit. In either instance, the young woman ends her relationships as a coping mechanism, long before she gets too involved with the other person.

Subsequently, when the tools a person has been accustomed to using in their life to explain why they feel a sense of fear fail them it may be time for them to seek out another path to resolve their issue and gain the assistance of a licensed therapist or Christian counselor.

Seek the Counsel of a Licensed Therapist or Christian Counseling

The effects of fear can be so overwhelming and cumbersome for a person to handle on their own that it might be necessary for some outside intervention to be included in their plan of healing. More than often, people, especially those within the body of Christ, tend to avoid the help of a licensed therapist or Christian counselor because it is thought to be something that believers should not do or the stigma that is associated with it. Even so, there is a myth which suggests that if a person is under the care of a licensed therapist or counselor then somehow, they must be mentality disturbed. But that is far from the truth. The rationale, however, for getting counseling is for the person to get to the root cause of their problem and to find solutions to better cope with it or get rid of them.

Confront Your Fear

It is with great certainty that once a person has begun their journey with the help of a licensed therapist or counselor in discovering the root causes of their fear in life, then the next best thing for that person to do is to find a way to confront the fear that has kept them from living a free and vibrant life. Like anything else in life confronting one's fears can be a difficult task to accomplish. For example, take a person who must admit that they have an addiction problem and their admission requires them to verbalize that addiction. In hindsight, admission of addiction by the person is an act of liberation but for the addicted person it may be viewed as an admission of failure.

Retrospectively, just as the person who is an addict must admit that they have a problem to move toward recovery, the same holds true for a person who is living with fear. It would be necessary for those individuals living with fear not only to confront it but also clarify what they are afraid of.

Depending upon the type of fear that a person is confronted with, it would be wise that precautionary measures are taken to avoid any further damage to the person's psyche or disposition and if possible to keep them away from any potential bodily harm. Although it is a challenge for those living with fear to confront it, the confrontation is necessary in the healing process. For this reason, the ability to confront one's fear releases the person from its grip and forces them to live out their life in a more productive way.

Challenge Yourself

Beyond the point of confronting one's own fears head-on, the next liberating move that should be taken into consideration in the life of a person who is attempting to rid themselves of fear is to move out of their arena of familiarity by doing something new and out of the norm. For example, Clara normally travels to work on a route she selected for fear of getting lost or being involved in an accident; suddenly she changes her route without knowing if the new route will get her to work in a timely manner, without getting lost, or having an accident. However, Clara's sudden change does prove to be beneficial to her. Clara's decision to change not only allowed her to arrive to work before her scheduled time, she did not get lost and arrived safely.

Although it may be difficult at times for people to change their habits and the way they have grown accustomed to doing things it may prove to be beneficial to them in the long run. Change is never easy, but it is necessary because you never know what new and exciting opportunities you could be passing up.

Express your Thoughts in a Journal

The last sensible solution that could be offered to anyone who is battling fear would be for them to purchase a journal to jolt down those things that closely resemble fear and attempt to invade their new walk in freedom. It would also be advisable that as those noticeable hindrances have been written down, the person would address them immediately and without hesitation. Additionally, it is suggested that the person draft a bucket list of things they would like to do in life but have been too afraid to do them. Then they should go out and do it.

Nonetheless, it does not matter what approach a person utilizes to eliminate fear from their life. It does matter, however, that they acknowledge what fear is and find the most appropriate course of action to take to escape the grip of their arch nemeses. Hence, the more a person attempts to rid themselves of fear the more they will be able to live beyond their self-imposed limitations and no longer coexist with this disruptive, manipulative, and unhealthy emotion. Instead they empowered to make a conscious decision to trade fear for faith. The trade-off, in the end, will prove to be more beneficial in life.

CHAPTER 6

Fearless Living

You may be wondering to yourself at this very moment, what does a life free from fear look like in a world filled with disaster, hate, and chaos? Well, the goal at this stage of questioning is to gather a substantive and reasonable description of what fearless living is all about. This task may be somewhat cumbersome because the depiction of a life free of fear for one person may not necessarily represent another person's portrayal of living free of fear.

Based on this assertion, here are a few suggestions on how a person can possibly live out life free of fear. From a biblical perspective a life free of fear resembles one of peace, a peace that surpasses all understanding; a type of peace that is maintained at a marginal level throughout times of adversity. It is noteworthy to mention that genuine peace only comes into a person's life after they have established a personal relationship with God through his son Jesus Christ.

Moreover, a life free from fear resembles one that is full of faith; it is encompassed with trusting and believing in the sovereignty of a merciful and kind God. For many people this way of life may seem to be a bit far-fetched, especially when they have lived a long-time enslaved by the demonstrative emotion of fear. Although fearless living may seem foreign and impossible to some people, it is within reach for those who constantly strive to obtain it. This statement is affirmed with the saying, *"that anything worth having is worth fighting for."* As stated in Luke 1:37, *"for nothing is impossible with God."* Therefore, anyone who desires to have a life free of fear must believe that it is possible and put forth the effort, in confidence, to secure it.

Living an adventurous life is another example of how some people can live out a life free of fear. A person of this caliber is unafraid and, to a certain extent, is daring and unrestrictive in nature. These individuals enjoy meeting different people and exploring new places. People who dare to live a fearless life do not accept the limitations that life may impose on them nor do they accept the word *"No"* as the end all answer to their requests. Consequently, a person who embraces a fearless life is always eager to discover different approaches to solving a problem, especially when they receive a *"No"* during the midst of resolving their issue.

To further expound on the notion of what fearless living consists of, let us consider the life of a person who no longer possesses a negative mindset; their way of thinking is realigned. Simply stated, there is no more *"stinking thinking"* embedded within the constraints of the person's mindset. [The realignment of this person's thought-process is two-fold: 1.) How they perceive what they are experiencing in life and 2.) How they respond to situations when they occur.] Moreover, the realignment of a person's mind-set leads to viewing life from a more positive light.

For the most part, fearless living involves the capability of a person to remain in the present without thinking about or anticipating what is to come. This line of thinking aligns with the *Theory of Mindfulness*. In an article written by Dr. Karen Wegela, it was suggested that Mindfulness embodies the practice of meditation by which an individual acknowledges what they hold to be true in their present state, moment by moment. [14] Although the theory of mindfulness is contrary to Christian belief, it does allow for a person to remain in the present moment and provides them with the opportunity to experience the transformation of their perception about a hopeless life to a life that is filled with high aspiration and enthusiasm.

Finally, for a person to live a life that is free of fear, it is important that they limit the amount of time that they spend on reading, listening and viewing negative words, voices or images daily. This course of action is imperative because the ears, eyes, and mouth are not only vital parts to the human body, they are the gateways to our soul. It is essential that we guard our ears and eyes at all cost; we must remain conscientious of the words we speak so that neither the wrong words are put in the atmosphere nor will the wrong information or images enter our spirits.

Ultimately, living a life free of fear encompasses the limitless will power of a person to see life without restraints and not view the challenges that may arise in life as stumbling blocks or obstacles but as opportunities that will elevate them to levels where greatness is accomplished in their life. Those individuals, who choose to live a fearless life, do so with the zeal and determination to do things that have never been done before, despite the opposing forces that maybe against them.

Fearless living only leads to living a life where there is nothing missing, and nothing is broken. A life free of fear incorporates the notion that a person has gained a renewed and rejuvenated faith and trust in Jesus Christ. Consequently, the resurgence of one's faith in God is essential to a long-lasting life of fearless living.

CHAPTER 7

Regenerated Faith

Once a person has made a conscious decision that they will longer live with or entertain the spirit of fear, it is then, with this realization, that they experience a paradigm shift in their spirituality, mindset, the way they live, and how they view the world around them. This type of shifting opens the door for the person's faith to be regenerated. For the most part, a regenerated faith involves the reconnection of a genuine relationship with God and fellowship with his son Jesus Christ. More importantly, a regenerated faith in God reestablishes an individual's trust in him and coveys a message that he is bigger than what they may have been afraid of in the past.

Despite that fear may try to overtake a person, a regenerated faith provides them with the courage and boldness to step out of their comfort zone and do something to help someone else. For instance, take the life of Moses, Exodus 3, who felt that he was inadequate when he was instructed by God to go before Pharaoh and demand that he let God's people go. Moses did not believe that he was capable of leading God's people out of Egypt once they were released from captivity.

Also consider Queen Esther, Esther 1-10, who at the urging of her older cousin Mordecai, risked her husband King Xerxes finding out her identity and the possibility of being put to death to save her family as well as an entire nation of people. A regenerated faith in God restores a person's confidence and affords them the opportunity to step out of the unfamiliar and into new experiences without a clear understanding of what the outcome may be.

Moreover, an individual's regaining their faith, or more so faith in God, is based on their decision to trust or not to trust. Let's revisit the Spiritual Pendulum Effect, this illustration provides an explanation of the importance of a person regaining their faith in God. The Spiritual Pendulum Effect shows us that we only have two options in life: 1.) to live in fear and not trust God or 2.) trust, believe and have faith in God.

No matter which option a person chooses on the pendulum, the choice they make will have a significant impact on their spiritual walk. For example, some people will reluctantly choose the path that leads to fear because they trust in their own senses and abilities. Meanwhile, there is another group of people who will choose the path that leads to faith. These individual's faith develops and grows even when they are confronted with difficulties and uncertainties in life.

Nonetheless, our decision to follow and trust God gives us the courage and faith to make it through any difficult circumstance that may arise in our life. Therefore, it is recommended that any person who is on the road to regenerating their faith in Jesus Christ, do so with the full reassurance and confidence that God is always faithful to those who would otherwise be deemed faithless. With that being said, faith in God is the only antidote to overcoming fear.

COMPLIMENTARY STUDY GUIDE

Scriptures to Eradicate Fear

There are over 365 text references within the bible that instruct us to not be afraid of anything. Below you will find a short list of scriptures based on specific categories of fear that have been gathered to assist you in your quest of eradicating it from your life.

Fear of the Future	Fear of the Unknown
Genesis 15:1	Mark 5:36
Deuteronomy 1:21	Psalm 46:2
Joshua 1:9	Mark 6:49-50
Isaiah 41:10	John 6:18-19; 14:27
Nehemiah 2:2-3	Psalm 23
Psalm 23	2 Timothy 1:7
Psalm 43:10	Romans 8:15
Psalm 71:1	Mark 4:35-41
1 John 4:18	Psalm 37:23-24

Fear of your Enemies	Fear of standing for Righteous
Deuteronomy 20:1	2 Timothy 1:8-12
1 Samuel 14:6	2 Timothy 4:5

Psalm 23	2 Timothy 2:3
Psalm 91	Ephesians 3:1
Proverbs 1:33	Romans 1:16
Matthew 10:31	Luke 9:26
Hebrews 13:6	Luke 12:8-9
1 Peter 3:13-14	Matthew 10:31-32
Psalm 34:7	2 Timothy 2:12

Fear of Success
Joshua 1:9
Deuteronomy 30:6-9
Matthew 6:33

Fear for your Family
1 Peter 5:7
Psalm 91:7-10
Proverbs 12:21

Scripture Reflection on Fear

Scripture:_____

_____

_____

Reflection:_____

_____

_____

_____

_____

_____

_____

_____

_____

Scripture:_____

_____

_____

Reflection:_____

_____

_____

_____

_____

_____

_____

_____

_____

Scripture:_____

_____

_____

Reflection:_____

_____

_____

_____

_____

_____

_____

_____

_____

Scripture:_____

_____

_____

Reflection:_____

_____

_____

_____

_____

_____

_____

_____

_____

_____

Scripture:_____

_____

_____

Reflection:_____

_____

_____

_____

_____

_____

_____

_____

_____

_____

Scripture:_____

_____

_____

Reflection:_____

_____

_____

_____

_____

_____

_____

_____

_____

_____

Scripture:_____

_____

_____

Reflection:_____

_____

_____

_____

_____

_____

_____

_____

_____

Scripture:_____

_____

_____

Reflection:_____

_____

_____

_____

_____

_____

_____

_____

_____

Scripture:_____

_____

_____

Reflection:_____

_____

_____

_____

_____

_____

_____

_____

_____

Scripture:_____

_____

_____

Reflection:_____

_____

_____

_____

_____

_____

_____

_____

_____

Scripture:_____

_____

_____

Reflection:_____

_____

_____

_____

_____

_____

_____

_____

_____

Scripture:_____

_____

_____

Reflection:_____

_____

_____

_____

_____

_____

_____

_____

_____

Scripture:_____

_____

_____

Reflection:_____

_____

_____

_____

_____

_____

_____

_____

_____

Faith Building Scriptures

Below you will find a short list of verses of scripture that have been complied for your convenience to assist you in the building of your faith. To gain a deeper understanding about faith, make sure to obtain to a study bible with a concordance.

Faith for Family

Genesis 50:24

Deuteronomy 3:16-18

Joshua 14:6-12

1 Samuel 3:8-9

Matthew 17:17-20

Mark 9:23-29

Psalm 128

Deuteronomy 31:12-13

Luke 15:11-32

Isaiah 6:8

John 6:47

Hebrews 12:14-15

Ephesians 6:16

James 2:14

Faith for Finances

Joshua 1:8

2 Kings 4:1-7

Matthew 6:33

Psalm 37:4;25

Deuteronomy 15:1-11

Deuteronomy 29:9

Matthew 17:20

Malachi 3:8-11

Genesis 8:22

Mark 4:26-29

Psalm 65:9-13

Job 42:10

2 Kings 6:16-17

Proverbs 3:9-10

Ephesians 6:1-4   Exodus 23:19

Faith for Health

Mark 6:53-56

Matthew 9:20-29

Mark 5:27-36

Luke 8:43-50

Luke 5:17-19

Romans 4:17-22

Matthew 15:16

Isaiah 38:16

Jeremiah 3:17

Jeremiah 17:14

Luke 4:40

Luke 17:19

Luke 18:42

Acts 3:16

Faith for Marriage

Psalm 119:125

1 Corinthians 13:11-13

Ephesians 5:21-33

Genesis 2:18

Malachi 2:14-16

Romans 7:2-3

1 Corinthians 7:12-16

1 Corinthians 7:27-39

Hebrews 13:4

Faith for Success

Psalm 37:5

Proverbs 3:6

Proverbs 10:14

1 Peter 2:24

Proverbs 12:15

Proverbs 16:3

Scripture Reflection on Faith

Scripture:_____

_____

_____

Reflection:_____

_____

_____

_____

_____

_____

_____

_____

_____

Scripture:_____

_____

_____

Reflection:_____

_____

_____

_____

_____

_____

_____

_____

_____

_____

Scripture:_____

_____

_____

Reflection:_____

_____

_____

_____

_____

_____

_____

_____

_____

Scripture:_____

_____

_____

Reflection:_____

_____

_____

_____

_____

_____

_____

_____

_____

_____

Scripture:_____

_____

_____

Reflection:_____

_____

_____

_____

_____

_____

_____

_____

_____

_____

Scripture:_____

_____

_____

Reflection:_____

_____

_____

_____

_____

_____

_____

_____

_____

Scripture:_____

_____

_____

Reflection:_____

_____

_____

_____

_____

_____

_____

_____

_____

Scripture:_____

_____

_____

Reflection:_____

_____

_____

_____

_____

_____

_____

_____

_____

Scripture:_____

_____

_____

Reflection:_____

_____

_____

_____

_____

_____

_____

_____

_____

Scripture:_____

_____

_____

Reflection:_____

_____

_____

_____

_____

_____

_____

_____

_____

_____

Scripture:_____

_____

_____

Reflection:_____

_____

_____

_____

_____

_____

_____

_____

_____

Scripture:_____

_____

Reflection:_____

_____

_____

_____

_____

_____

_____

_____

_____

Scripture:_____

_____

_____

Reflection:_____

_____

_____

_____

_____

_____

_____

_____

_____

Scripture:_____

_____

_____

Reflection:_____

_____

_____

_____

_____

_____

_____

_____

_____

ENDNOTES

[1] James Strong. "Daag." *The New Strong's Complete Dictionary of Bible Words*, 344. Tennessee: Thomas Nelson Publishers, 1996.

[2] Robert B. Costello (Ed.). *"Fear."* The American Heritage College Dictionary. New York: Houghton Mifflin Company, 1993.

[3] W.L. Walker (2014). *Fear.* Accessed June 15, 2016,

http://www.biblestudytools.com/dictionary/fear

[4] *"Faith and Fear."* Merriam Webster Dictionary.com-Unabridged. Merriam- Webster Incorporated. Accessed June 10, 2016,
http://www.merriam-webster.com/dictionary/fear

[5] "Fear." *Psychology Today*. Sussex Publishers. Accessed June 13, 2016,

http://www.psychologytoday.com/basics/fears

[6] *"Faith."* Dictionary.com. Collins English Dictionary-Complete & Unabridged 10th Edition. HarperCollins Publishers. http://www.dictionary.com/browse/faith (accessed: March 7, 2018).

7 Ledbetter, Sherry. (October 13, 2015), commented on "The second wave of the Chapman University survey of American fears," *Chapman University* (blog), commented October 13, 2015, https://blogs.chapman.edu/press-room/2015//10/13/what-americans-fear-the-most

8 Jeffrey Winters. "Why we fear the unknown." *Psychology Today*. May 1, 2002, https://www.psychologytoday.com/articles/2002005/why-we-fear-the-unknown

9 "Depression." *Anxiety and Depression Association of America*. Last Modified August 2016, https://www.adaa.org/understanding-anxiety/depression

10 Sheldon G. Sheps, M.D. "Can anxiety cause high blood pressure?" *Mayo Clinic.* Accessed May 9, 2018, http://www.mayoclinic.org/diseases-conditions/high-blood-pressure/expert-answers/anxiety/faq-20058549

11 Krista O'Connell. "Insomnia concerns." *Healthline*. Accessed July 11, 2016. http://healthline.com/health/insomnia-concerns#overview1

[12] "Social Anxiety Disorder." *Anxiety and Depression Association of America*. Last Modified August 2016,https://www.adaa.org/understanding-anxiety/social-anxiety-disorder

[13] Julie Warren. "Does Exercise Release a Chemical in the Brain?" *Livestrong Foundation*, June 2, 2015, http://www.livestrong.com/article/320144-does-exercise-release-achemical-in-the-brain/

[14] Karen Kissel Wegela . "How to practice mindfulness meditation: Mindfulness is important; how do we develop it?" *Psychology Today*, (blog), January 19, 2010, https://www.psychologytoday.com/blog/the-courage-be-present/201001/how-practice-mindfulness-meditation

CONSCIOUS OF THE HEART PUBLISHING, LLC

Upcoming Publication

Girlfriend I Forgive You

A Young Woman's Journey to Wholeness

A Novel by Bessie Stewart-Banks

www.ingramcontent.com/pod-product-compliance
Lightning Source LLC
Chambersburg PA
CBHW071418040426

42445CB00012BA/1211